9781646710607

Gentle Creatures
Wisdom Deck

By Dan May
Written by Arwen Lynch-Poe

Copyright © 2021 U.S. GAMES SYSTEMS, INC.
All rights reserved. The illustrations, cover design, and contents are protected by copyright. No part of this book may be reproduced in any form without permission in writing from the publisher, except by a reviewer who wishes to quote brief passages in connection with a review written for inclusion in a magazine, newspaper or website.

10   9   8   7   6   5   4   3   2

Made in China

Published by
U.S. GAMES SYSTEMS, INC.
179 Ludlow Street
Stamford, CT 06902 USA
www.usgamesinc.com

Introduction

The Gentle Creatures welcome you to their world. Here in this realm of deep forests and vivid landscapes, you will find a tribe of gigantic bipedal folk who want to walk with you. Commune with each member of this tribe to learn from them, laugh with them, and even rest your head on their soft furry shoulders. Each one is an individual with a heart, mind, and soul of their own. From gray to black to white to auburn and more, their fur color is an autumnal-hued quilt. Each creature sprouts horns that show a myriad of directions. From the youngest creature to the oldest and wisest, all celebrate their individuality by intentionally using non-specific pronouns. Rather than a family of he's and she's, they prefer they and their because it reminds them that they are not separate from one another.

Hold out your hand. A Gentle Creature will greet you with love and honesty. Rather than abrupt, definitive statements, they prefer to allow your own instincts to have sway. Each card carries a message for you to absorb, then use as you see fit. In the world of Dan May's furry folk, humans are welcome as long as they approach with open hearts and minds.

Emotion is made atmospheric in Dan May's Gentle Creatures series. A quietude fills these spaces—instants that feel like defining interactions for his fuzzy giants—and wisdom and curiosity are in balance. Facial expressions might be hidden from view, but body language reflects the drama of life, and the artist is sure to include a "glimmer of hope even in the saddest of moments."

May describes his art as "not from a specific time or place; it is surreal in nature and puts forth suggestive themes that can lead the viewer toward a unique story." In turn, each story is outlined by its setting and often grounded in the natural beauty of northern Michigan, where the artist lives and works.

The Gentle Creatures

~ All ~

When you are worried about your place in the world, remember this Gentle Creature. Standing in the midst of a starry sky, they gaze intently at their own palms. What is contained within the space of two hands? How can any of us capture what the universe truly holds for us? It can be an overwhelming question, can't it? You could journal on the question of "what is all" in so many ways. Perhaps this is a reminder that we are all. Just that. All. None of us are any less valuable than the next member of our tribe. When we consider that our tribe consists of everything, like our friend in this card, we may find ourselves contemplating our own worth. For those times that it seems to be more than we can hold, take a step back. Sit down. Feel your own root extending deep into the earth. Press your spine against something firm like a tree or a friend. See your own head opening up to thrust up a ray of light that goes on and on and on into the sky. Repeat the following to yourself. "I am all. I am enough. All is all." Chant the words as you feel everything expanding outward. Hold on to the feeling of being one with everything. When that feeling fades, start from the beginning. Look around you, dear one. Who else needs this message? It is your turn to remind another that they, too, are All.

Beacon

Three creatures brave the rising water to make sure everyone has been alerted. They stand back to back knowing that together they can be a brighter beacon than alone. Their patience is rewarded by one lost straggler finally finding its way home. Had they not stood there under that stormy sky, the bird might have been lost. The lesson here is that when things look dark, find friends who believe as you do. Then do the work necessary to make sure all are safe. Without the sturdy feeling of each other, this trio might have given up. It is not easy to hold your ground when angry clouds loom and the water is surging. A question for you to think about here is, "What must I stand up for? Who will stand with me?" You can be a better beacon knowing that others have your back. Don't despair if you are feeling lost. Look for those who brighten up your life.

Clearing

Sometimes we all need a little help. Our Gentle Creature is getting that help. They have had so many rough spots, so many hurts, that they needed to take the time to rid themselves of that negativity. They watch as a feathered companion removes their burden. Our friend here used a bit of folk magic. They held the egg in the palm of their hand. Taking time to really think about their most recent journey, they spoke to the egg. This card is about putting your fears, your worries, your anxieties into the egg. Then it can be carried away by you or someone else to be let go of in a caring fashion. Do not imagine yourself broken if you find yourself filled with thoughts that are darker than you like. Instead, let yourself acknowledge that these are things that happen to all. It is necessary to release them rather than let yourself be weighed down. You can always call on your most trusted friend to help you with this clearing of your burden. Do note that you are not always the one who needs to unburden yourself. Sometimes, you are the one summoned to help another as their most trusted friend. This is a notification to go within yourself. See which role you must take on today. It is okay if you sit with a friend as you both clear the air and yourselves.

Conjurer

Under the full moon of the seventh moon, the Conjurer waits. They have taken up the prayers, entreaties, and pleas from the people. Now they must send those requests up to the sky to be answered as the Universe wills. Our Conjurer knows a secret though. As much as they pass along this ancient knowing, most never take heed. So they must commune with the owl, nature's messenger. This bird helps by taking up each application for benediction. It returns time and time again until all the hopes and wishes are dispersed. Now it returns to the Conjurer, the village holy one, to share a meal and a warm fire. When you see this card, the message should be clear. When you have need of someone to hear your worship, your wonderings, your worries, remember this one key thing. Once you have done your asking, hush. Be silent. Remember that you have two ears and one mouth so you can listen twice as much. Many of us never allow the Universe to answer us. We keep talking right over the messages. Or we deny the answer. This is where just pulling another card is not the best thing to do. Sit with the image. Stay in the moment of the message. Do not allow your self to get in the way of what the Conjurer brings you. Magic is yours. Be silent and listen for a while.

ᗰ Connections ᗩ

Our Gentle Creature has taken a moment out of their crazy day to just sit for a while. They have been rewarded with a visit from a delicate denizen. These two are old friends who have not had the time recently to just stop and connect. Or maybe it would be more honest to say that neither of them has made the time for their friendship. This pause to check in with each other is as necessary as watering a houseplant. Nothing thrives without intentional moments of caring. So they will spend this interval catching up. Maybe over laughter…maybe over tears. Either way, they are honoring the work that it takes to nurture their personal bond. When this card shows up, remember those friends you haven't heard from lately. If you haven't heard from them, have they heard from you? Connecting with others is a two-way street. Never waste your energy on those who are not willing to do this work with you. You are worth the time it takes to build real connections.

ᗡ Cosmos ᘖ

Our gentle friend asks a simple question. "Where is my place in the cosmos? Who am I?" The winged messenger doesn't bring an answer. Instead, it brings a key on a red cord, which represents the circle of life. The key is what will unlock the answer. The key doesn't unlock any specific mechanism of iron or steel. Instead, it unlocks the mystery of all parts of the cosmos showing where each of us fits in. Each of the cosmic orbs represents a place of learning that our creature must visit. The lesson here is that there is no one place where the creature or any of us belongs. We are all made up of multiple and complex potentials. We are all complicated varieties of a set of skin and bones that can miraculously hold space in more than one realm. The question is not so much 'where' as it is 'how many wheres?' The beginning of the quest of the cosmos is also the end of the quest. It is a circular riddle that continually answers itself.

ᗯ Create ᗢ

Sometimes you must create your own fire. This Gentle Creature was in need of flame. They had to cross this river on a dark night with the moon hidden by the clouds. This was a journey they couldn't avoid taking. Belief in the power within is the message they carry. Even when they are at their lowest, they have a clear knowledge that this ability to make things is always within them. You may feel as if your own talent to bring forth your imagination has lapsed. Trust in your own internal flame, seeker. It may be that you need this time of living without that flame. It teaches us what life is like when we are disconnected from our authentic selves. This creature is willing to share their igniting spark with you. Reach out. Let this card jumpstart you. Embody that creative flicker within. Pick up pen, paintbrush, potting tools, or pans. It's time to execute that complex series of steps that is your unique dance. Make it known to the world that you are here to give birth to those wild and free ideas within your soul. Create a beautiful moment. Then create another and another. Remember that your own sparks will leap out to ignite another who feels like you do. That is the gift of creating.

Curiosity

Curiosity woke up this Gentle Creature. For too long they had meandered through life without purpose. One day they came upon an unusual plant. No one else knew anything about this plant. Our friend took it upon themselves to learn everything they could about this green denizen of the woods. As they worked with the first plant, they became aware of another and another until suddenly their life was full of growing things. They learned so much that others came to them to be taught. By simply being curious, our Gentle Creature moved from a life of wandering aimlessly to one of work, knowledge and teaching. You are being given the opportunity to learn something new right now. Let your own inquisitiveness find those unexplored areas. Pack up your notebook, your pen, and anything else you might need. This is a call to satiate that thirst for knowledge. Feeling like a refresher course? Needing to go deeper? This is your time. Join our friend studying their plants by setting up your own lab or field station. Indulge your inner student by buying a book on that particular subject. Can't find that book? Maybe it is time for you to commit to paper and share with others what you have discovered from following your curiosity.

🐦 Daybreak 🐦

Daybreak dawns as the adventurers prepare for another day. Birds take off to show them the way for today's journey. It is time to face a new set of challenges. They understand that the way they begin isn't actually the way they must end. For them, they avoid locking themselves into someone else's patterns. Should they have an argument in the morning and hold onto that until nightfall? No, this group understands that our days are not run by hot words. Rather, the way they go forward offers them chances to grow even more. So they welcome the soft glow of this new day. Promising one another that the most urgent thing is to tackle obstacles to move beyond rather than lug more baggage around. Challenge yourself to start each day as a promise rather than a problem.

🐦 Directions 🐦

Here are two creatures whose paths have crossed on this starry night. The crescent moon doesn't offer a lot of light but the stars lend their own glow. The barn owl has asked the Gentle Creature a question of direction. The Gentle Creature crouches down to listen closely. When someone asks for guidance, it is often good to know more about the individual. Does the owl wish to fly there as many would assume? Or is the owl planning to travel in short hops, remaining close to the ground? Once those matters are clarified, then directions can be given. In return, the owl offers the Gentle Creature answers to their own questions about the road ahead. Directions can be funny things. Sometimes they place us on the direct path. But often they offer us a chance to explore more. And that extra path can mean the difference between a destination and an adventure. What do you want when you ask for directions? Are you looking to reach the end or to discover something new?

Drift

Two Gentle Creatures relax as the waves carry them along. They lean against one another secure in the knowledge that the support they need is there. They've been paddling hard for so long but they know that rest is as important as the work. The red sail is full with a leading wind so they are confident that they are going somewhere. The butterfly is also drifting along behind them. Sometimes it lands on their face during the hardest times just to remind them that a chance to drift is coming. Of course, they can't always drift can they? But this is not the moment to worry about that. Indulging in the quiet warmth at their back, each creature ponders the joy of doing nothing at all. They are in the moment. And that is harder than one might think. This card asks you how you are drifting right now? If you are constantly struggling and not making progress, it may be a good time to let the elements take over and do their work, while you simply breathe. Maybe a butterfly on your nose would help you realize when it's okay to just drift along for now.

⇝ Effort ⇜

Every now and again, you just need to put out the effort. Our lovable creature holds up a small umbrella. It is evident that this umbrella is not going to do any real good in terms of the falling rain drops. The yellow slicker the young girl wears provides more protection. But the fact that the umbrella is offered shows that the creature cares. They themselves are not bothered by the rain, but know their smaller counterparts can sometimes be adversely affected by too much cold and wet. So, as they say, "Mama tried." Or in this case, "Creature tried." Here is a reminder that we need to keep trying to do the right thing. Even when it is too little, it is noticed. The need to be kind is the most important thing. This card is a reminder to ask ourselves, "How can

I show someone I care today?" Reach out in good faith. Help someone whenever you can. Your efforts will be noticed.

Family

Family is a funny thing. It is not always chosen, but it is always a matter of love. Here we see a couple welcoming a newborn into their unit. The two younglings tugging on the branch demonstrate that togetherness doesn't mean we all pull in the same direction all the time. Being a member of a core group brings you the best and worst of things. You always have someone there to stand up for you and with you. Their loyalty is a thing of true endurance. However, you will also have those who know you well enough to call you out when you mess up. The blessing is that they won't abandon you after they tell you what you did wrong. They will be there as you work to correct your mistake. Family goes both ways. Whether it is chosen or blood family, take a moment to honor your own community. As you have been there for them, they will be there for you. Ask yourself what family looks like to you.

Friendship

In troubling times, it's hard to remember that we are not alone. Here our creature contemplates the moon. They are feeling so lost in thought that they have not heard the soft booted footsteps of the small person beside them. But once that connection is made, that hand to hand contact, our creature is gently pulled back to the here and now. They are reminded that they have a friend. It is this commitment of companionship that returns them to a more balanced way of thinking. Now, they have someone to talk with. It is that gift of quiet listening that we all need. For this card, ask yourself, "Who do I need to talk to about this?" or "What point of view am I missing here?" Never fear that you are alone in this world. We all have someone who will always be at our side. Cherish them. Let them know how much they mean to you soon.

⤳ Gift ⤝

Here our friends both gaze at butterflies. They are focused on the beauty that rests so lightly on their fingertips. Both know a secret that they are willing to share with you. When you receive this card, ask yourself if you are truly enjoying what is yours? Or do you sometimes furtively glance at someone else, thinking they have something better. Or worse, that they are better than you. The gift these two companions share is special, but not the same. How can she look at her butterfly in the same way the Gentle Creature looks at theirs? Who can say which butterfly flies with more grace or holds more charm? Once you realize that no one can do any of those things, you will begin to approach a place of true joy. Comparing yours to someone else's is a good way to fall into a hole filled with a wanting that cannot be filled. Instead of comparing with envy, look at what you have. Celebrate the unique being that is yourself. When you hold out your hand to share rather than to grasp, you become the person you were meant to be. What can you do today to connect with love rather than envy? Each of us is special. Don't dim your own light because it doesn't shine in the same way as someone else's. If you must compare, compare the person you are now to the person you were ten years ago—or even yesterday.

Groove

Find your groove! Shake your tushie! Grab some crazy friends who will dance with you even if there is no music. Here our Gentle Creature puts the needle to the vinyl. Ants wave four limbs in anticipation of the song to come. Whatever your song is, move to it. Car dance, chair dance, whatever movement you can manage is called for here. You are being asked to break out of your routine to take a moment to wiggle wildly. When we let go with abandon, our hearts are free to sing as loud as they like. So turn it up! Now is the moment you've been waiting for. Let the whole world see how you can bust a move as you choreograph a whole set of steps for your brilliant life. Dance to the music. It's time to get down and get groovy.

Guardian

The job of guarding infinity is no small thing. Three watchful guardians observe as our gentle friend contemplates the bottle that holds the infinite light. This is the source of all sacred things for the world. Within the bottle lies hope along with sorrow, fear along with courage. It is all things to all creatures. To be asked to be a keeper of this light is an immense task, but one that this youngling has accepted. When you accept the task of caring for something, you take on a similar role. Each part that we play is woven into the greater whole. You are being asked if you are ready to assume the mantle of guardianship in some new way. Only you can know the answer, but remember this—there will always be others helping. You will never be alone in this work.

Guide

Our Gentle Creature waits patiently holding the lantern aloft. Their job is to guide others in through the foggy night. It may sometimes be a lonely job to serve as the light carrier, but it is a necessity that cannot be shirked. They understand their part in the fabric of the community they call home. Not all are called to be guides, but this one was. The hardest thing about being a guide is that not all will see or appreciate the illumination for what it is. How many notice the fairy dancing within the lamp, creating the flickering glow? Look closely. What do you see? With this card, you are being asked to be a guide or to answer the call. One way or another, your journey is being redirected. Are you heading into the fog ignoring the sparkling flame? Do you feel as if you are waiting forever for one person to see your light? This is a time to really dig into your inner self. It can be that both of these things are important. After all, it is a poor guide who cannot be led. And wouldn't it be sad if this Gentle Creature were left to hold that lamp? Surely there is someone, maybe you, who can help them by carrying that sweet yellow star for a while? We all need to both guide and to be guided.

Harbinger

A light beckons us forward. Bats swirl around this harbinger, but what news do they bring? Numbers tumble down. Seven is the number of seeking, of thinking, of moving forward on a quest. Nine marks its territory as selfless and compassion. Our creature then is showing us that a new journey awaits. The bats may come from our own internal dark place. Rather than scary, they are simply helpers. The numbers are also gifts to you. Study them. Learn about them. Be compassionate with yourself as we were all beginners at some point. And we will all be beginners again. Follow the path of inquiry currently calling you. Open your eyes to see what light is in front of you. This isn't a time for delay as the call to the journey is now. While you may want to plan more or think things through, you need to do that en route. Ask yourself what you actually need in this moment. Perhaps you can grab a pen, a snack, and a journal. All else that you require will be found. Some journeys are long while others are short. But when you receive this signal, follow the signs. You will be rewarded for your trust.

Harvest

"When shall we make our pumpkin pie?" The young Gentle Creature peers down at their friend, the spider. The response is not what they hoped for. "There is time, my friend. There is time." Impatient as many younglings are, our questioning friend wants to know why. The spider waves a few legs around as it talks about proper timing. Rushing a harvest results in sour, bitter, tough results. This is a thing that must be patiently planned for. Rushing in to snatch up all the orange orbs won't make the delicious pie as hoped for. Instead it will be spongy rather than firm and green rather than golden. No amount of nutmeg, cinnamon, and allspice would fix that. While there are things to be made with unripe pumpkins, our Gentle Creature learns that if they want the tasty dessert, they must wait for the harvest to be ready. What are you rushing? Have you considered how your hurrying may yield results no one will find satisfying? Learn from the spider that knows how to wait in its web. Timing is everything at this point.

Heal

Our two friends share a quiet moment. The larger one has come to ask for a blessing, a healing. The woman has donned her priestess' robe to meet them at the cliff's edge. Too often we imagine we are alone. Instead of reaching out to ask for what we need, we pull back. Remember that even the tiny mouse helped the lion. Whether you are miniscule or mighty, what's important is the act of asking. That is far more urgent than anything else here. Remember that healing is something best shared. You never know when your pain can help someone else through their own grief. Perhaps it is a loss so great you fear your heart might break. Maybe it is a fear rooted so deeply within your soul that it has become like a second self. You are at your strongest when you can say, "Please, I need your help." Trust that you will find the person who can help you heal. Trust that the one who can help you will. Allow those who can't, help their own space to heal. You are at the edge of the cliff either asking for benediction or giving it. We all must hold sacred both those roles. Will you be the mouse or the lion today? Don't worry. It will change as necessary.

Heard

Have you ever felt like no one hears you? Even when you sit perched on a barrel waiting for the coming storm, will there be someone who has a moment to listen to your fears? Sometimes that is a small someone you may have not noticed until now. Sometimes it is someone taking the time to come out of their own shell to let you know they are there to hold space for you. Our friend has climbed up on his perch by using old tires. They have been calling for help into the wind only to hear their own voice blown away. So much sadness can only be contained by letting it go into the fierce gale that sends those clouds scudding across the sky. Fearing everything, they cling to their seat wondering why they even try. Then they hear it. The small, soft "Hello friend" of someone who cares. That is the moment when they understand down to their very cellular level that everything will be okay. When you feel unheard, remember that you do matter to someone. That person hears you. How can you be that quiet voice for someone else in your life?

Invitation

"Let's be playmates! You can climb the stairs to look out over the world with us." Our two Gentle Creature younglings have created a marvelous tree house for themselves and have dreamed up all kinds of imaginative activities. But they don't want to play by themselves so they have issued an invitation to their friends. One has answered their playful call, eager to see the wondrous things higher up: the big fluffy clouds and delicate little butterflies. The new arrival has been welcomed and encouraged to climb the stairs and join the others. Hang over the balcony to enjoy the expansive view. Look up and see the sky through the leaves and branches. Scramble through the rooms! This is an invitation to be part of something new and unknown. All you need to bring is your imagination and your enthusiasm. The most enticing invitations are the ones when you never know what will happen next.

Key

A forest dweller offers a key to our seeker who wears a similar face. This Gentle Creature has been practicing a type of shamanic magic called shapeshifting in some cultures. They wanted to understand what it is an owl truly sees. How does an owl feel just watching in the woods? Our friend did the work, becoming the owl as much as they could. Now they don the mask of the owl to show that the lesson has been learned. They thought they knew what the lesson was. But that lack of humility had them sitting in the woods much longer. For the real teaching was the lesson of non-judgmental observation; seeing the owl fly low and not adding to the story by interpreting its intentions. Being with the owl as it dozed in the tree rather than imagining what the owl was thinking. This key to this valuable life-long lesson is to open yourself up to receiving information without preconceived ideas about what it all means. Do not set up boundaries for yourself or anyone else that predetermine choices. The gift you give and get when you just open up to the moment is a lifelong one. Once you have this key in your hand, you will forever be in that space of observation, seeing everything as it is, through fresh eyes.

Kindred Spirits

When is the last time you had a cuppa with a friend? Tea, coffee, water—it doesn't matter what is in the cup. The gift lies in the holder of the handle. That is the true joy of the moment. Whether you gather to remember a friend, a moment, or to plan a new adventure, make time to chat. This isn't a deep discussion between our two here. She's stopped by on a whim. They've shared their beverage with her. This spontaneous moment in a field is a gift they share. Rather than check the time, they gaze into each other's eyes. This is intimacy that cannot be forced or manufactured. No one is judging them on how they look or what they choose to talk about. You are being shown how to anchor yourself in this moment. If you don't have a convenient meadow to wander in, reach out to someone. Perhaps call that friend you haven't spoken to in a while. Maybe it will be someone you see every day. Whomever it is, give yourself the present of being present. You might speak to a stranger just to tell them you like their hat, their smile, their shoelaces. Isn't it lovely when we can take a break to have a chat with another person? Do that today.

Listen

How do you effectively reflect on what someone is saying to you? How can you make sure you are hearing their heart through their words? One way is to actively listen. That is the art of concentrating on the words being spoken. We have to make a conscious effort to engage on all levels. When we are actively listening, we are offering a gift of self. Here, two creatures visit by the water's edge. One is sharing how they feel about this spot and its importance to them. The listener who holds their heart in their hands is being fully present for this reflective conversation. They are fully aware of this significant moment. A hummingbird hovers overhead. It has been attracted to the energy of this heartfelt exchange. Perhaps a good thing to examine right now is who listens to you in this way? To whom do you offer this present of being present? When you need someone to truly hear what you are saying, make sure you are that authentic listener for them as well.

Loss

Grief moves among us like a figure in a foggy river. This Gentle Creature mourns the loss of his winged friend. Even knowing that the moth had a short life cycle, there is still the feeling of loss. Losing someone to death, distance, or disagreement leaves an empty space inside. This card illustrates that everyone mourns in their own way. One turns away to gaze into the coming light, hoping for another winged beauty. The other looks directly at the moth remembering the beauty of its dancing gold wings. Each is right. Let no one tell us how to grieve our losses—even the ones we know had to come. Lean into your emotions to let them flow through you. Sadness will not end you. Rather, it will wash out pain so you can begin to honor what was. What is remembered lives. You will move on from this point carrying the good memories with you.

⤫ Meet ⤭

A flight of brilliantly blue budgerigars startle at the sight of this Gentle Creature. They have taken wing in a panic. But because this creature has simply stopped, the curious little birds begin to mill about. You can almost hear them twittering to one another about this stranger. Who is it? What is it? What is its purpose? Will it hurt them? As they flit around, they begin to settle down. One even swoops so low it can look up into the eyes of this immense being. In our world, we have all been both stranger and part of the flock. No matter which side you may be on right now, remember how it feels to be on the other side. What was fearful to you once may be as common as dirt. Do you remember that first day at a new school? Where others might have swirled around like these bits of feather? Or when that new person walked in to the office. Did you gather with those familiar to you to discuss this newcomer? It is a natural thing.

When this card shows up, ask yourself what is causing your own "Budgie response." Take time to learn enough about someone or something so that what was once strange turns into a familiar sight.

～Nurture～

When you hold something precious in the palm of your hand, there is a feeling that almost overwhelms. You want to nurture it. You want to provide it with safety and security, with the knowledge that it is unique in this world. Our own hearts are like this. Our creature is wrapped in the embrace of their own arms. They know that the most valuable thing in their lives is themselves. So the energy reflected here is that marvelous act of caring for ourself as if we were truly marvelous. For we *are* truly marvelous. We deserve this energy as much as anyone else. The more we cherish ourselves the more we can nurture others. But when we allow ourselves to be wrung dry, the only thing we can offer is a brittleness of spirit. When is the last time you put effort into nurturing your own soul as though it were the most precious gift?

༺ Offer ༻

Our two friends in this card have taken a moment to meet under the full moon. The soft glow lights up the forest. There is an ambiance of quiet that allows our Gentle Creature to be fully engaged in accepting the gift his young friend has offered. It may be a handful of random green things to someone else, but to her, it is something she chose with great care. Her friend understands that. The gift for them is not what is in their hands but what is in the heart of the small one looking up at them. They are both grateful for one another. Honoring one another with their full attention is another gift given in this space between companions. Have you given this to another recently? Do you need more of this in your life? The present is here. Focus on the air around you. Smell the scents. See the sights, hear the sounds. If you offer yourself up to each moment as a gift, you will learn the beauty of being present in the moment. What requires your presence? Perhaps it is time to turn off all other things to spend time with someone who needs your undivided attention.

Past

Along the way in life, we are gifted so many things. Here, on a tandem bike ride, one friend looks ahead to keep both riders on track. The other looks behind to see what's behind them. He is greeted by the sight of a friendly bird hurrying to catch up with them. When we remember to examine our surroundings, what amazing things we find. It is all well and good to focus on the future, but we should never forget friends and experiences from the past. The questions you might want to ask yourself with this card are, "What lessons from my past can help me right now?" and/or "Who am I forgetting from my past that could possibly help me in my current situation?" So pedal toward the future, but always consider what is behind you. Buried in that past are small treasures of memories and people who will still be there for you.

Pause

A caesura is a break in a verse where one phrase ends and the following phrase begins. In music, this break may vary between the slightest perception of silence all the way up to a full pause. In life, this is the moment you are given to assimilate what has just happened before being taken into the next experience. Our musical creature has set his instrument aside to enjoy the beautiful flower his music has conjured up. Rather than just look at it, he immerses himself in the experience by smelling it, holding it, and gazing into the very center of this bloom. Consider how you approach the pauses you are given in life. Do you pace restlessly waiting for the next action? This card is showing you that perhaps it is time to sink into the quiet of right now. Allow yourself to be present by engaging all of your senses. How does this moment feel to you on all levels?

⋙ Peace ⋘

Even when the sky seems stormy, there will be moments of peace. Set your heart toward finding them. Always follow that stray butterfly just to see where it will lead you. A moment of reflection is what is called for at this time. If someone or some situation has riled you up to the point of not seeing clearly, it's time to not just smell the roses, but to actively seek them out. By doing this, you will create a small space where you can regain control of your thoughts and emotions. Peace may not last forever in our harried world, but take a lesson from this card. There is always time to fuss and bother with all the many things we have to do. But only you can carve out those mind-easing moments of peaceful contemplation. When this card appears, ask yourself this. What can I do to invite more peace into my life?

Play

Look at these happy young Gentle Creatures. They are being pulled by an adult. A butterfly keeps landing on their noses. Shrieks of laughter spread joy as they go wheeling into the meadow. Now is not the time for work or hard things. Put down your implements of work. Follow the young ones. Let them lead the way for you. It is in this moment that you need to play. Move your body. Aim your heart for the playground you miss. Do not allow anyone to tell you that you are being irresponsible when you take a moment to sink yourself into the mindset of a child. Play is as important as work. No dull Jacks here, please. Freshen your outlook by jumping in puddles, swinging on tires, or napping under a tree. Maybe you can't get outside? Not to worry! These young ones will remind you that building a blanket fort is ageless. Having marshmallows and graham crackers are as tasty inside as outside. Swing your arms. Do whatever you can to open yourself up to the playful spirit. By doing this, you will find the answers that have been evading you. They are like butterflies landing on your nose—a tickling nudge. You know the questions can be resolved. The knotty problems will unwind. Once you get out of your own way, all things will get better. So let loose and frolic, friend.

Quest

Under the glow of the full Scorpio moon, our Gentle Creature has undertaken their own quest. They have the lamp with the phoenix feather to light the way while their belt carries potions of healing. The dagger is made for helping others rather than causing harm.

The mask is a symbol of their work as a guide, a shaman. But they are not done. Even though they have all the tools of the healer they are, there is always another level to attain. They have been taught by their own teacher creature that one must always learn more. So this creature has set themselves a task. They are off to see what the world wants them to learn. Perhaps you could try this as well. Rather than asking to learn a specific thing, you might pose the question "What does the universe want me to know today?" It can be a powerful thing to let that float out as you let your heart loose to hear the answer that is waiting for you. The key here is not to force the response. Your job, like the guide's job, is just to follow the call.

Quit

There are times when you have to walk away. Call it quits when you have truly given your all to something, but have gotten nothing in return. This is an imbalance that you should not maintain. Look to those who are with you, not to those who fly away. Your true friends will point out when you have been throwing a tiny bucket on a raging flame. Quitting is sometimes the correct path. Especially when you are the only one fighting. It can be a place where you recognize that your effort will be best put elsewhere. Martyring yourself for a cause is one thing. Flinging yourself into the fire alone is another. Pulling back to regroup is definitely something you need to consider. Perhaps you can save someone else later. But for now you must quit trying to be all things to others and simply focus on saving yourself. Throwing in the towel isn't always a bad thing.

Risk

By taking the next step, our Gentle Creature moves into the unknown. They have spent all of their life behind this threshold. While it has always been easy enough to step over, this creature has never wanted to take the risk. Others have encouraged them saying, "It's an opportunity!" But there were those who whispered, "You never know what is out there. You might never come back." Finally, the impetus to go has overtaken the fear of failure. This creature has packed their things into a bag marked with the infinity symbol. In their heart they are pledged to the journey. It is with a light heart and a joyful outlook that they embark on this adventure in front of them. This card asks what adventures are calling you? How are you going to commit to your purpose? Sweep your worries away. It is time to move beyond your comfort zone. Expansion is the name of this game. Stretch your heart as you follow the call to become your next best self.

Road Trip

With the wind in their hair, a cozy couple sets off on a road trip to somewhere. They haven't decided where they want to go because they know in their happy hearts that the destination isn't as important as the company. In this case, their small winged friend who has been invited along gets to determine which way the wind will blow them. He isn't a navigator so much as an instigator. All three are traveling light, with no maps and no expectations. They are taking their time, so they don't miss anything. They are ready for everything! Where will your adventurous heart take you next? Who will ride beside you? Take these lessons from the Gentle Creatures to heart. Remember that you can choose the direction or let the direction choose you. The same goes for those who would travel with you. Sometimes you want a tried and true friend along for grand adventures. Other times it's exciting to find the courage to venture out alone and trust the winds of fate to invite new acquaintances to join your journey.

ཙ Secrets ནྭ

"Put your head closer" she whispers to her friend. "What I have to say is secret." She quietly murmurs her words knowing they will be kept in the vault that is her confidant's heart. This is her way of unburdening herself when the world fills her too full. At those times where her head pounds and her heart aches, she can call her companion who will take in all of what she needs to let go of. It doesn't burden the creature. Each little gleaming firefly is carrying off a word here, a phrase there. The secrets will be spread throughout the woods until the time comes when this beautiful fairy has need of them. In return for this listening, she answers their beckoning as well. She will bend her head close to listen to what needs to be heard then watch as the glowing winged ones scatter the creature's word as well. You may have secrets that are pulling you down. Perhaps it is time to find that one who will hear you and help you. It is no weakness to trust another with your secrets. And remember...secrets don't have to be painful. They can be whispers of "you mean so much to me" "thank you for always being there for me" or "I appreciate your friendship." Consider who needs to hear your secrets. Call them to share with them. Then offer to hold theirs as well.

Spontaneity

Never miss an opportunity for fun. If there is a chance to make a big splash, take it. Maybe lately you haven't been reaching out to take advantage of offers from others. Here's a reminder that it is a very good thing to say yes to some playful time. Find a friend who needs the same shakeup in their lives. Then make it an adventure. Remember that time, like water, is ever moving. You miss the moment when you say, "Later" or "I'm too busy." This card reminds you to get ready for some impromptu fun. It may be only a small thing, but the memory will always outlast the moment. Ask yourself this, "What have I said no to in the past that I've regretted?" "What is holding me back from shouting yes to this offer?" You are allowed some spontaneity in life. Do not short yourself on moments of delight. It can buoy you through some other times in life where you just need to pull from the memory of this moment.

Stories

We all have stories to share. We all want someone to listen to them as much as we need authentic tales from them. Here two friends have taken the time to just get away from everything else. Now they enjoy the company of one another. In a perfect world, we all have someone who will listen to us. That companion who will simply hold space for us as we share our innermost thoughts. Then we will proffer them the same sacred act of listening to them with out judgment. We can all create this marvelous place. It may not be inside a tent lit by a lantern. It may not be in the deepest part of some ancient forest. Wherever it is, the gift we can offer to one another is to simply hear each other's stories. When you share your story with authenticity, you return that gift.

≽ Support ≼

Join our Gentle Creatures as they support one another. From the one resting on the ground to the one perched on their back, these two know what it means to be there for someone. It is less about knowing why they need you and more about showing up when asked. They remain gentle with each other because support isn't requested unless it is truly needed. One even rests their eyes as they are there simply for the job of being present. They are not needed for advice, input, critique, or anything other than their presence. This is a gift that is harder to give than we might imagine. How often have your requests for support turned from silent witness to Mr. or

Ms. Fix-It-All? Remember that when you are asked for support, it is always a smart idea to ask, "What kind of support do you need?" Some will need handholding. Some will need anything from a gentle boost to a swift kick in the rear. It is our right to ask for what we need and our responsibility to give what we are asked for once we have agreed to something. So don't let your own need for support hold you back from asking. You deserve it. Just set boundaries on exactly what you need. Our Gentle Creatures bring this lesson forward to you now.

Teacher

Come sit with the Teacher, the ancient forest dweller. So much has passed before their watchful gaze. They've seen birth, growth, death so many times. Understanding passages of time is their gift to us. When it feels as if something is taking too long, gaze into their eyes. Let their herbal smoke waft around you to remind you that time, like smoke, dissipates easily. The message they bring us today is one of dichotomy. Sometimes the act of waiting feels like dragging yourself through the thickest mud. Other times, you feel as if you are being propelled by hurricane-force winds. But time is a funny thing. When we dread something? When we do our best to ignore the coming event? That's when the hurricane blows. When we want something so badly? When we feel a desperate need to arrive at that next point? Mud, mud, mud awaits us. Will we be sucked down? Will we be blown away? Our Teacher creature offers this thought. What if we simply continued to move forward as we always have? Perhaps the lesson we need to contemplate today is that of living in this moment. If we focus on what is right in front of us, all things will happen as they are meant to happen. When we learn not to push the river or try to stop the wind, we can relieve ourselves of so much. Sit here with the Teacher a bit. Let yourself breathe and just learn.

ᗍ Turn Back ᗌ

Our Gentle Creature has turned away from the girl offering to share her light. With the creature's back turned on even the brilliance of the moon, they cannot see past their own gloom. Will they continue to move into the unknown and the unseen? They appear to intentionally not listen to their own heart whispering, "Turn. Turn. Turn." When we are deep within a place of sadness or hurt, it can be difficult to find a way to realign ourselves. This card offers an opportunity to pause. Let the softness of the moon and the sweetness of the gift offered guide you back to a better place. There is no need to assume that your actions taken while consumed by sadness and grief make you anything other than a being who has been hurt. Turn back. Apologize. Take the light and take her hand. Let the companionship of a silent, understanding friend comfort you in this time. All you have to do is turn back. Your only obstacle is within yourself. Turn. Turn. Turn.

Uprooted

Kneeling in a field of familiar flowers, this creature studies a handful of roots. They have been called to another field far from this one. With some regret, some sadness, they contemplate the meaning of roots. There is also a sense of hope here. They know that this field has been home for many seasons, but by taking this small bundle of roots, they will be able to plant a new place for themselves. It will not be this one, but they will be able to create something for others that also has roots and connections. By embracing this feeling of being uprooted, they can fill themselves with hope instead of dread. The unknown is waiting for them to answer the call. Their own love of home will never be forgotten. They are simply answering their own internal GPS pointing them towards a new future they hadn't considered until just this moment. Ask yourself how uprooting yourself has brought you to where you are. Follow your roots back to recall why you chose to move forward. Being uprooted isn't the worst thing in the world. Sometimes you are being given the opportunity to spread out in new ways.

Wait

Here our gentle friend has had enough. They have turned away from their friends and family to go off by themselves. But one small hand tugs at their finger. This touch is enough to make them pause. When we are overwhelmed by life, we often have the same reaction. Just wanting to throw our hands up in the air as we turn our backs to everything that has frustrated us. When the world seems to come down on you all at once, what is your initial response? This card is asking you to wait just a moment. Take some very deep breaths. Now take some more. There is a reason you are at this point. There's time to decide, but first you need to make sure you are present in the moment of now. You have those who care for you so connect with them. Pay attention to the smallest tug from someone you may have overlooked. Now is not the time to make any rash decisions. Instead, find that boon companion who is your own small voice of reason. Your next step is a very important one so honor your journey by not reacting from a place of hurt and anger. Take the time to ensure you are making the best choice for yourself first.

Wings

What a wondrous gift our Gentle Creature has been given. They have spent so much time studying and caring for their delicate-winged friends. Now they are rewarded with wings of their own. Wings to lift them into the air so they can swoop and swirl with their butterfly friends. Knowing the life cycle of these antennae angels has led them to do everything they can to help. From planting milkweed and other plants their caterpillar selves love, to providing a safe haven with all the flowers they love, this one creature has made a difference. And, what this creature doesn't realize yet, is the wings that spontaneously sprouted from their own shoulders didn't actually come from the butterflies. Those wings grew from the beauty of their own soul. Wings are something we all have. When we do those things for others out of nothing but kindness and love, we are developing our own wings. While we may not see them as easily as we see the ones in this card, know that they are there. Do not think they are something others have. You are two steps less from spreading your own wings. Your actions are on target to lift you higher. Flutter your wings within your own soul. Be the beauty the world knows you to be.

Wonder

Our gentle astronomer gazes through a telescope to see into the field of silvery wanderers above. A bird keeps company listening to the words of awe and wonder that come forth. Deep into the night, they watch the cosmic lanterns dance across the black velvet of the sky. They are amazed every time they see a new star. The ones they see every time inspire them to continually seek into the inky depths of space to see what new friends they might find. When is the last time you approached your life with wonder? Let the beauty of a wildflower growing unexpectedly awe you? It is time to examine your own soul. Go out to wander this vast land. Let yourself look at life with open, loving, bewilderment for a time. Not everything has to make sense. It will all unfold. That's the promise of the cosmic wanderers we call stars.

The Gentle Creatures Spread

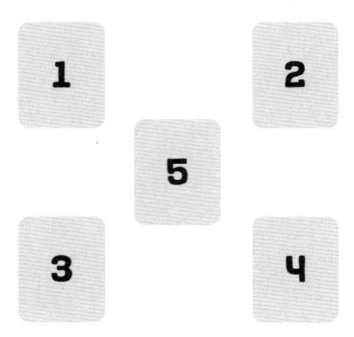

```
    1           2

        5

    3           4
```

Let the Gentle Creatures help you with a spread designed to show you how you can be kinder to yourself and to others. We often forget that the most important person in our world is ourselves. We work so hard that we lose sight of the goal—to simply be healthy and happy. Here is a five-card spread that offers insight on how to find ways to ease gentleness into our lives. Each card offers thoughts on how to regain a softness that may have been lost along the way.

Card 1: How can I bring more gentleness into my life?
Card 2: How can I let go of things that I worry about more than I should?
Card 3: Who can I turn to for nurturing and comfort?
Card 4: Who needs more nurturing and comfort that I can offer?
Card 5: What is the most important thing to know in this moment?

Priorities Spread

| 1 | 2 | 3 | 4 |

Here is a simple spread to help sort out priorities. So often we worry about things that may not need worrying about. A technique I developed is to ask myself Is It Important? (I.I.I.) and How Important Is It? (H.I.I.I.). I even have a small index card that I keep on my desk that asks 'I.I.I.?' If yes, 'H.I.I.I.?' I use this for remembering what is truly important. Sometimes, situations seem out of control. We've all had that co-worker, or been that co-worker, who comes running in with their hair on fire because something has gone WRONG. It's hard to remember to take a breath, step back, evaluate, and then respond. The Gentle Creatures are experts at helping us learn where we need to focus.

Card 1: TAKE A BREATH
Card 2: STEP BACK
Card 3: EVALUATE
Card 4: RESPOND

Take a Breath asks, Is it important?"
Step Back asks, "How important is it?"
Evaluate asks, "What is my lesson?"
Respond asks, "What is my answer?"

About the Artist

A native of Rochester, NY, Dan May began drawing and painting before age five. Dan attended Syracuse University where he studied illustration and began to explore new techniques, new media, and new worlds, particularly that of the pop surrealist movement. He achieved a BFA and began to immediately pursue his artistic interests. Dan considers himself a modern narrative painter who weaves a rich texture of the surreal and mysterious into his highly original flowing style. His detail-intensive works have become widely recognized for their dreamlike ability to transcend the natural states of space and time. His paintings have been exhibited internationally in galleries and museums. Dan lives and works in northern Michigan with his wife, Kendal and their three children.

About the Author

Arwen Lynch-Poe lives in enchanting New Mexico. She is an author of fiction as well as non-fiction. She is the past president of the American Tarot Association as well as the past owner/editor of *The Cartomancer* magazine. She has authored numerous decks including *Field Guide to Garden Dragons*, *Elle Qui Oracle*, *Fairy Tale Lenormand*, *Secrets of the Mystic Grove*, *Practical Tarot Wisdom*, as well as co-authored *Bianco Nero Tarot*. She is a professional tarot consultant who is known as the Professional Joy Seeker. She enjoys crocheting, backgammon, and readings.

Notes

Notes

For our complete line of tarot decks, books, meditation and yoga cards, oracle sets, and other inspirational products please visit our website:
www.usgamesinc.com

Follow us on:

U.S. GAMES SYSTEMS, INC.
179 Ludlow Street
Stamford, CT 06902 USA
Phone: 203-353-8400
Order Desk: 800-544-2637
FAX: 203-353-8431